DRAW 50
FAMOUS
CARICATURES

ALSO BY LEE J. AMES

DRAW 50 FAMOUS CARICATURES

Lee J. Ames and Mort Drucker

DOUBLEDAY

NEW YORK LONDON TORONTO SYDNEY AUCKLAND

PUBLISHED BY DOUBLEDAY,
a division of Bantam Doubleday Dell
Publishing Group, Inc.,
666 Fifth Avenue, New York, New York 10103.

DOUBLEDAY
and the portrayal of an anchor with a dolphin
are trademarks of Doubleday,
a division of Bantam Doubleday Dell Publishing Group, Inc.

Library of Congress Cataloging-in-Publication Data

Ames, Lee J.
    Draw 50 famous caricatures / Lee J. Ames with Mort Drucker.—1st ed.
        p.   cm.
    Summary: Step-by-step instructions for drawing caricatures of fifty famous people.
    1. Cartooning—Technique—Juvenile literature. [1. Cartooning—Technique.
    2. Portrait drawing—Technique. 3. Drawing —Technique.] I. Drucker, Mort. II. Title.
NC1320.A44   1990
741.5—dc20   89-48616   CIP   AC

ISBN 0-385-24629-3
        0-385-24630-7 (lib. bdg.)

Copy 1

To Mort, you're the greatest.

And to the Berndt Toast Gang
from which we hail.
—L.J.A.

TO THE READER

For many years I've had the pleasure of sharing my drawings with you—and my way of making those drawings. Recently some of the Draw 50 books have included the work of other artists as well. I've chosen artists whose work I've admired greatly. When they agreed to work with me I was delighted and so, it seems, were my readers.

Mort Drucker is considered by many to be one of the very best caricaturists in the country, if not THE best. In fact, actor Michael J. Fox once said, "I knew I had made it when Mort Drucker drew me." If you are half as pleased as I am, you will consider this book an exciting addition to the Draw 50 series.

When you start working, I would recommend you use clean white bond paper or drawing paper and a pencil with moderately soft lead (HB or No. 2). Keep a kneaded eraser (available at art supply stores) handy. Choose the caricature you want to draw and then, very lightly and very carefully, sketch out the first step. Also very lightly and carefully, add the second step. As you go along study not only the lines but the spaces between the lines. Size your first steps as closely as possible to the lines and the spaces in the book—not too large, not too small. Remember, the first steps must be constructed with the greatest care. A mistake here could ruin the entire drawing.

As you work it's a good idea, from time to time, to hold a mirror to your sketch. The image in the mirror frequently shows distortion you might not have noticed otherwise.

In the book, new steps are printed darker than the previous steps. This is so they can be clearly seen. But you should keep your construction steps very light. Here's where the kneaded eraser can be useful. You can use it to lighten a pencil stroke that is too dark.

When you've completed all the steps, and when you're sure you have everything the way you want it, complete the drawing with firm, strong penciling. If you like, you can go over this with India ink (applied with a fine brush or pen), or a permanent fine-tipped ballpoint or felt-tipped marker. When your work is thoroughly dry, you can then use the kneaded eraser to clean out all the underlying pencil marks.

Always remember that even if your first attempts at drawing do not turn out the way you'd like, it's important to *keep trying*. Your efforts *will* eventually pay off and you'll be pleased by what you can accomplish.

My sincerest hope is that you not only develop drawing skills but that you enjoy creating these caricatures and have fun in the process.

LEE J. AMES

TO THE PARENT
OR TEACHER

In fourth grade, many years ago, we were given an assignment to draw something to honor President Lincoln's birthday. An immediate competition developed among the four or five class artists. Which of us could draw the best portrait of Honest Abe?

We, of course, would not agree that any other one of us did the best. Our pride led each of us to consider himself the winner. Today I couldn't honestly make the judgment call that mine deserved to be number one, but I did learn something that ultimately resulted in the Draw 50 books.

I learned the importance of peer approval. The encouragement given to us artists by the rest of the class and the praise we gave each other was heady inspiration. Most of the group went on to become successful professionals.

All the drawings of Abraham Lincoln that the class artists made were copied from other sources. This despite general disapproval of "copying." We copied from the Lincoln penny; from a five-dollar bill; from a calendar; and from sale advertisements in the newspaper. We copied someone else's work, stroke by stroke, and we erased and reworked. Many considered this to be a noncreative, harmful way to learn drawing. But we liked what we finally got. Our friends and classmates liked what we did and we were encouraged. We were on a roll, and that was of overriding importance.

Later we were able to learn technique, theory, media, and much more with the gift of incentive provided by friends, classmates, and family. Early on we copied, then we found ways to do our own original things.

Mimicry is prerequisite to creativity!

It is my hope that my readers will be able to come up with drawings that will bring them gratifying approval. After that I look forward to the competition.

Enjoy!

LEE J. AMES

Draw 50 Famous Caricatures

ARNOLD SCHWARZENEGGER

OLIVER HARDY

STAN LAUREL

JACK NICHOLSON

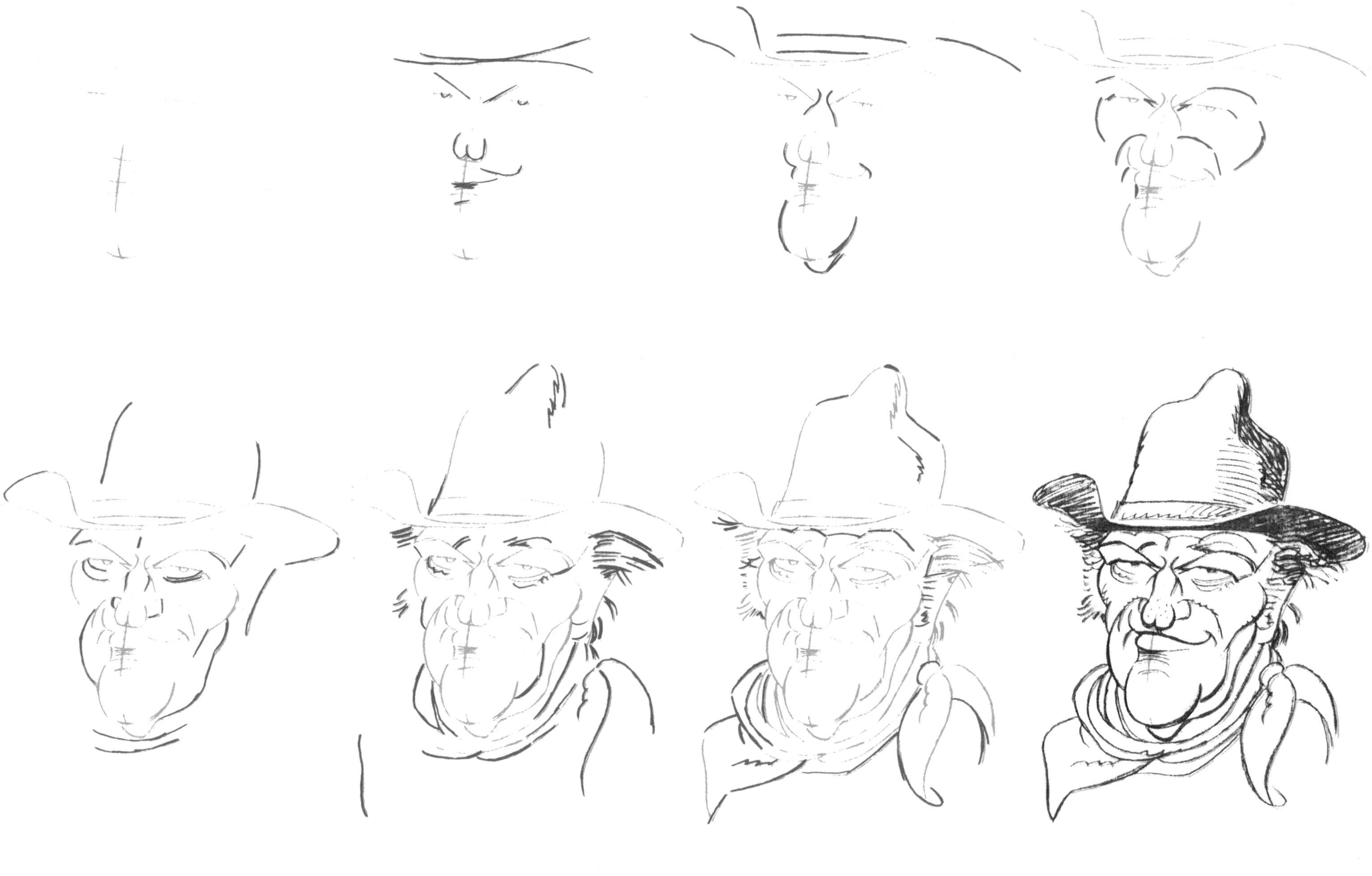

JOHN WAYNE

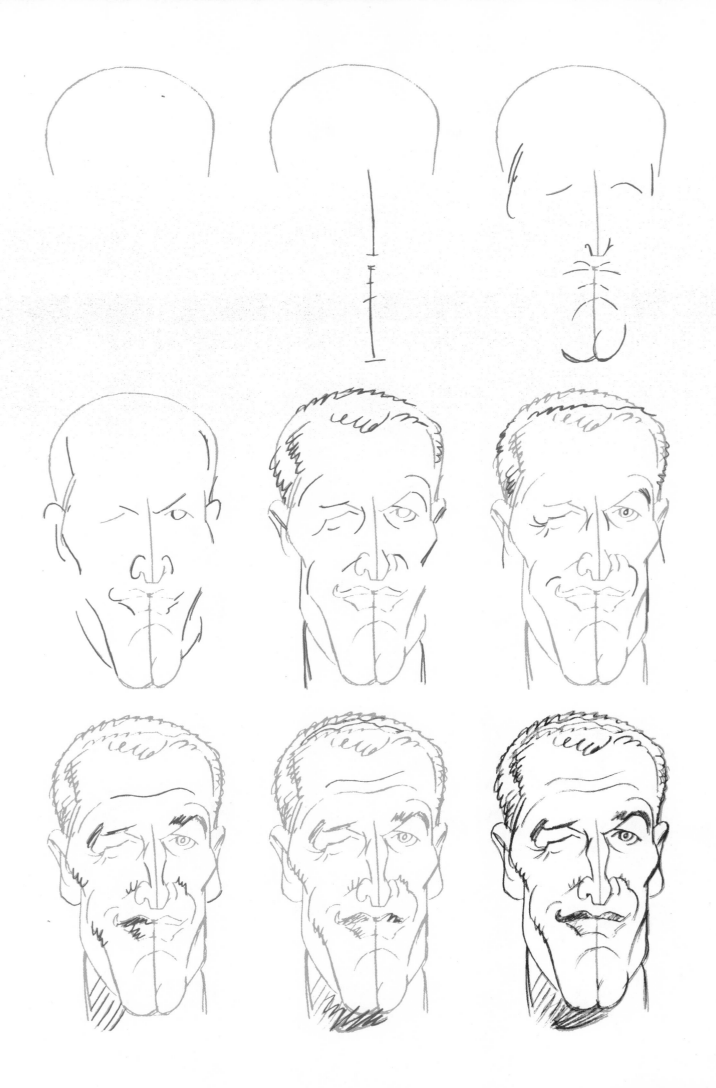

PAUL NEWMAN

MICHAEL J. FOX

DOLLY PARTON

MERYL STREEP

RONALD REAGAN

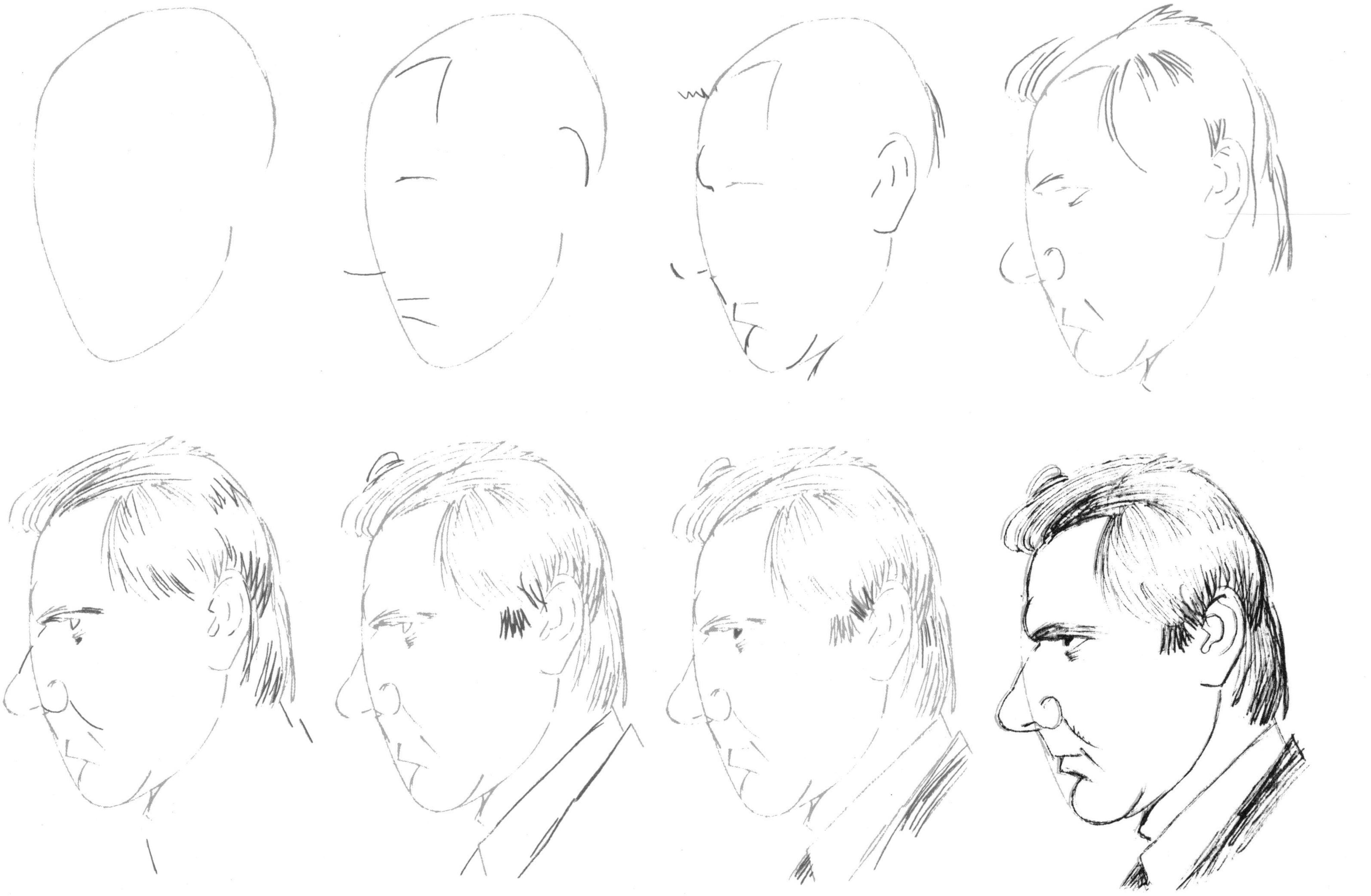

HARRISON FORD

MOE

SYLVESTER STALLONE

BRUCE WILLIS

LIZA MINNELLI

WHOOPI GOLDBERG

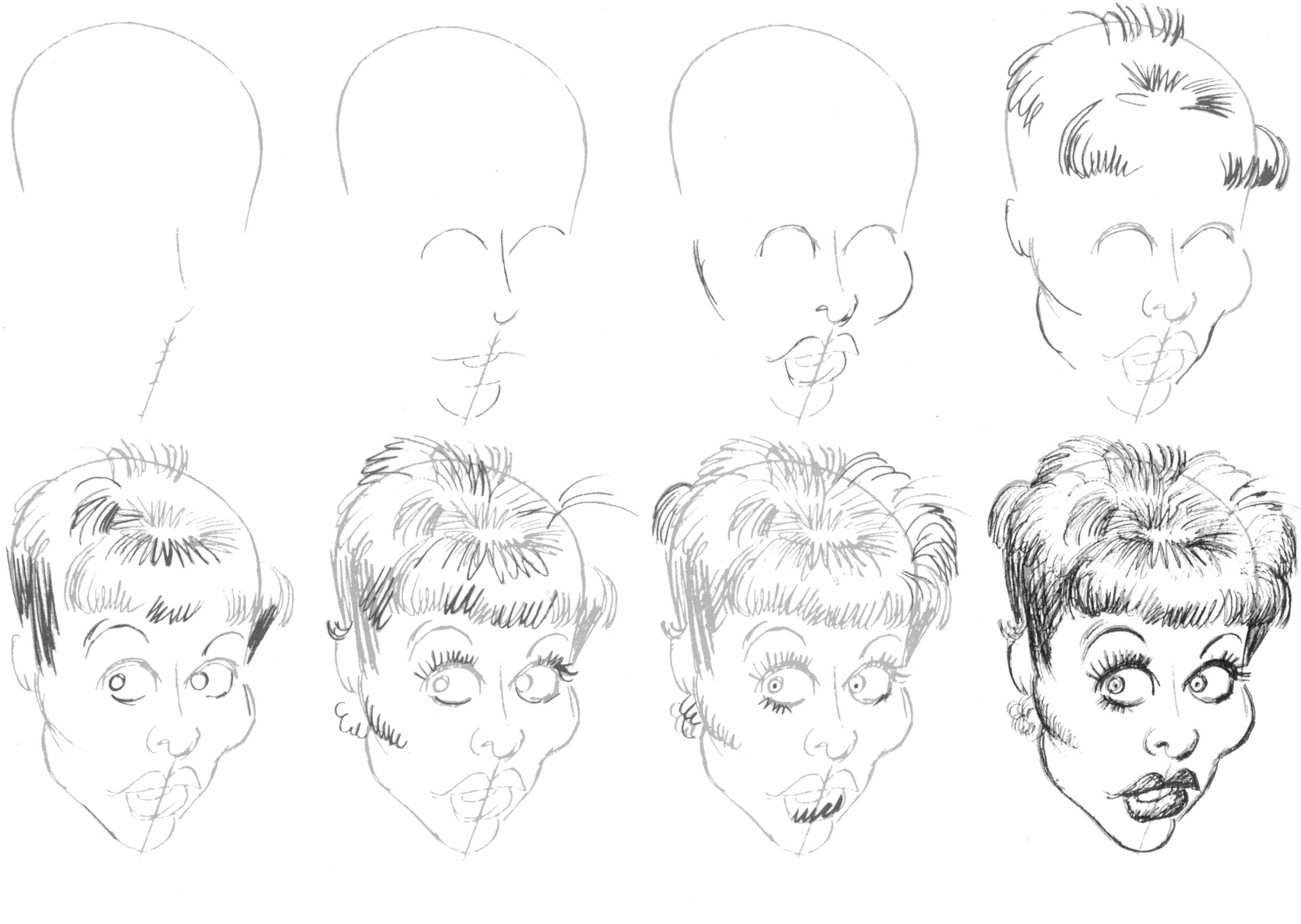

LUCILLE BALL

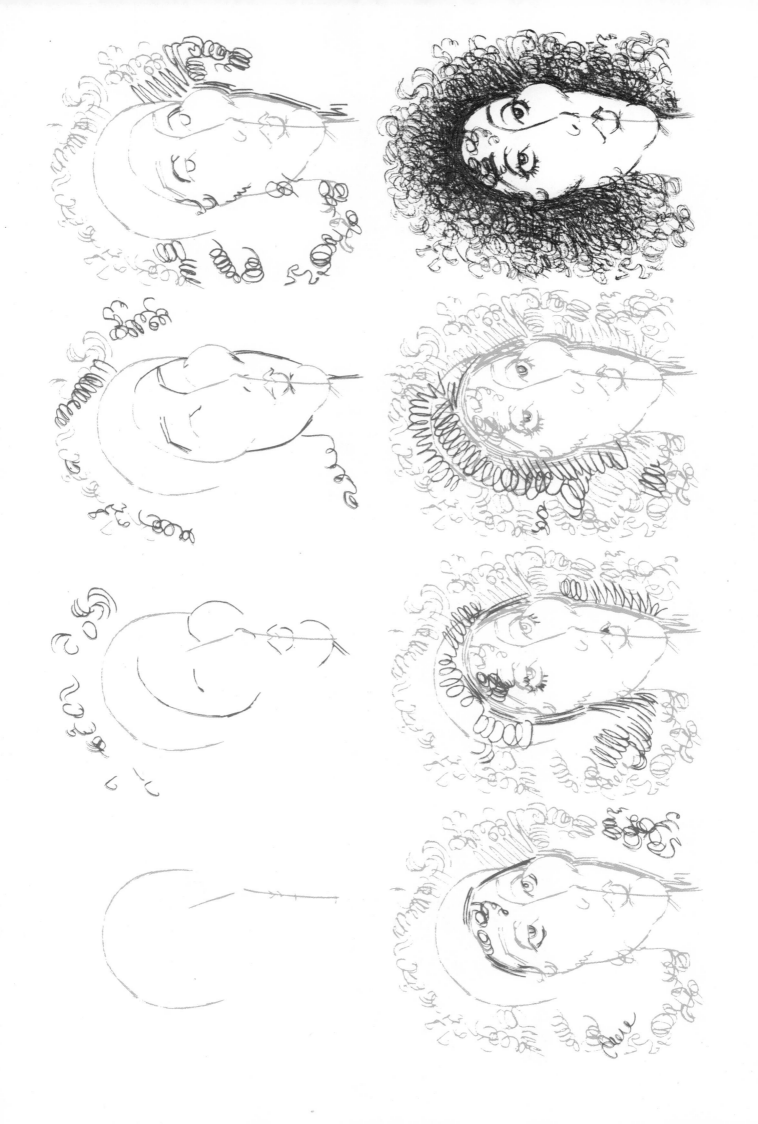

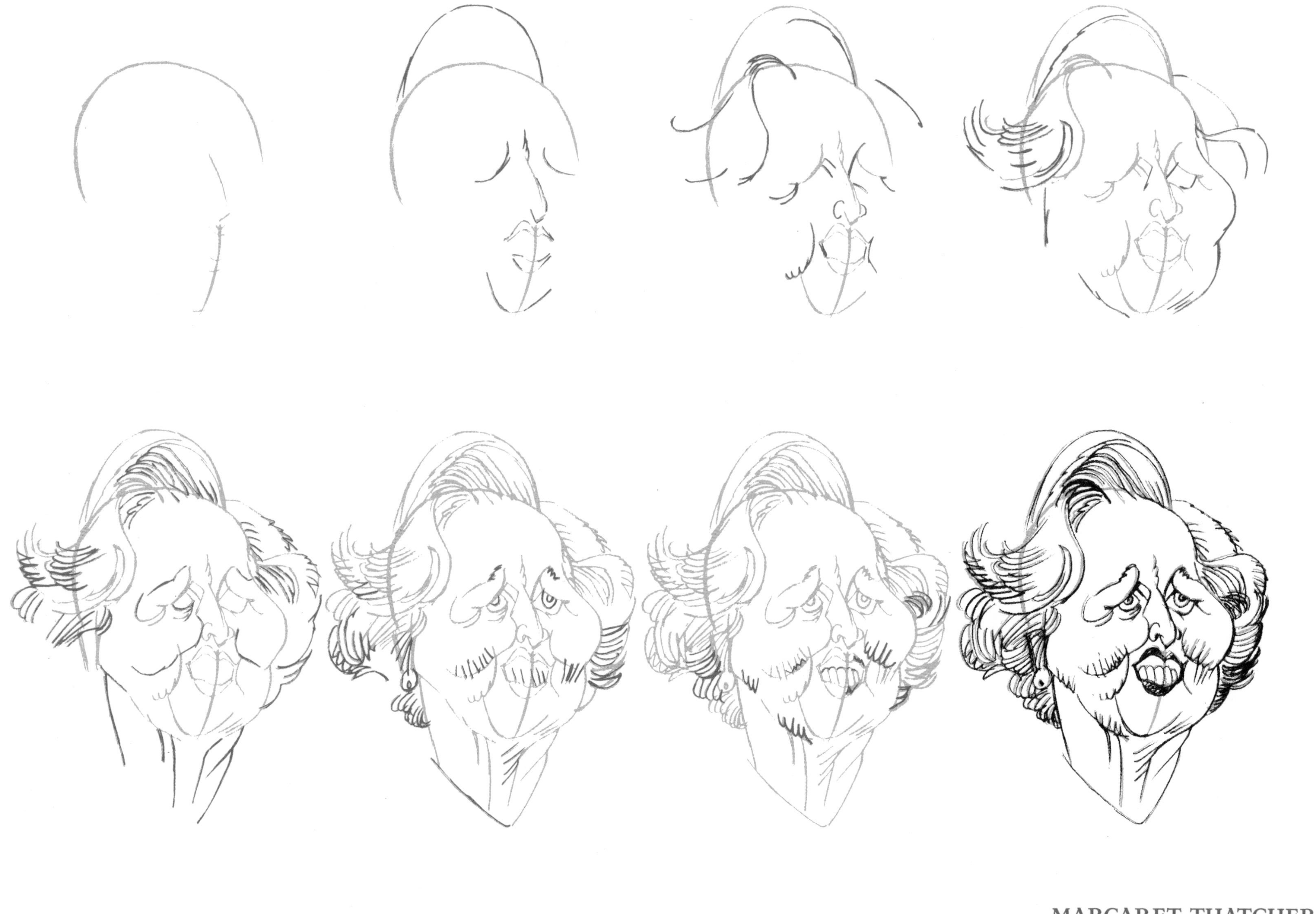

MARGARET THATCHER

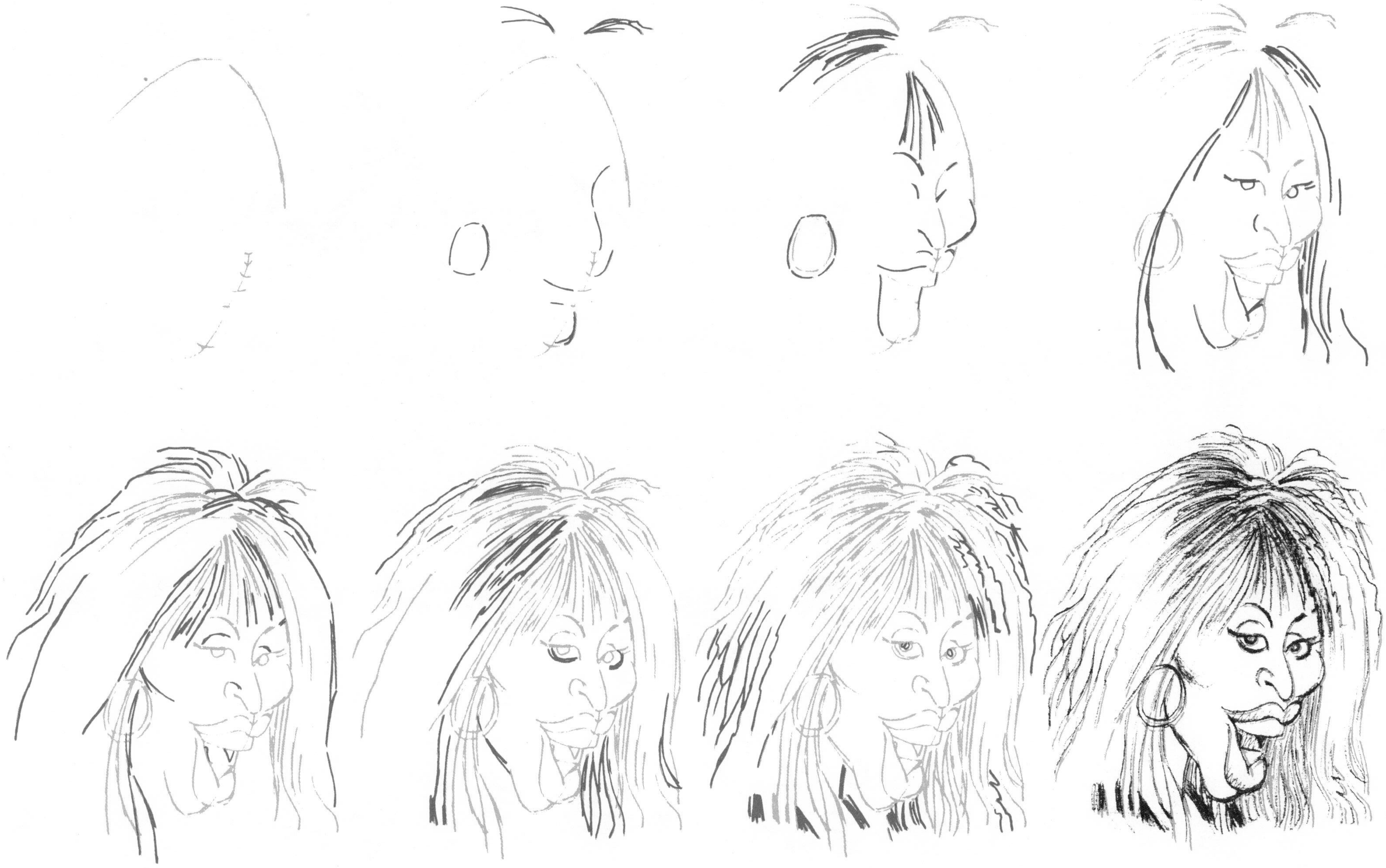

TINA TURNER

MATT DILLON

ROSEANNE BARR

DIANA ROSS

MICHAEL DOUGLAS

LILY TOMLIN

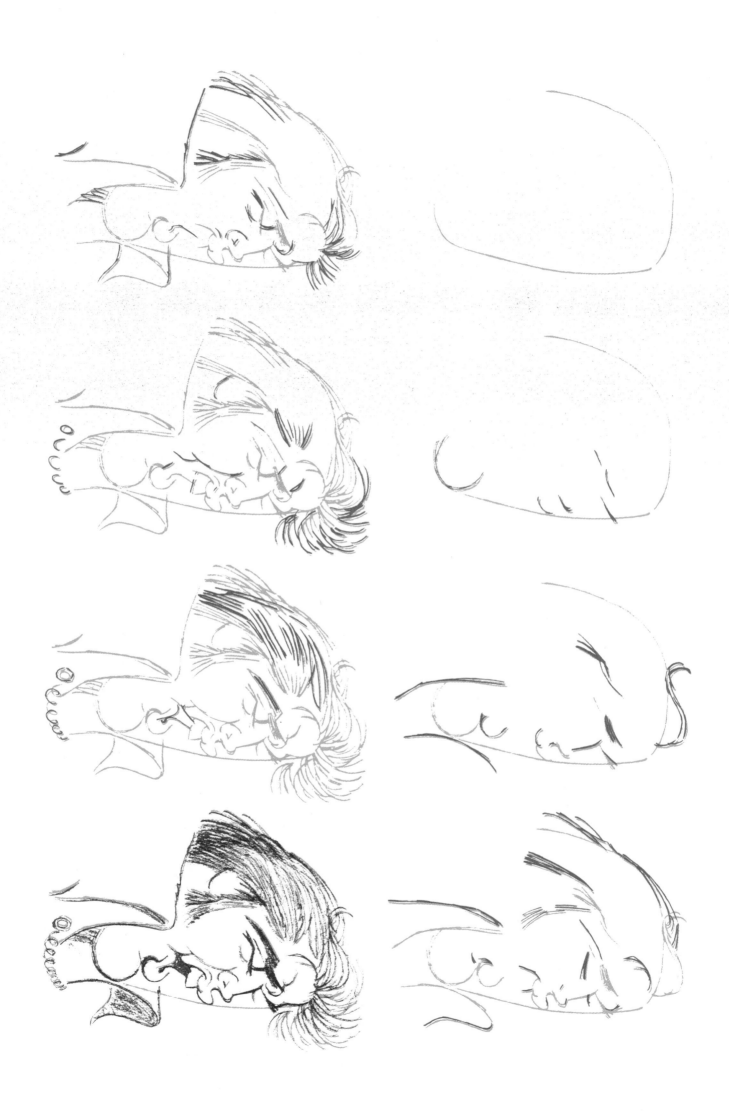

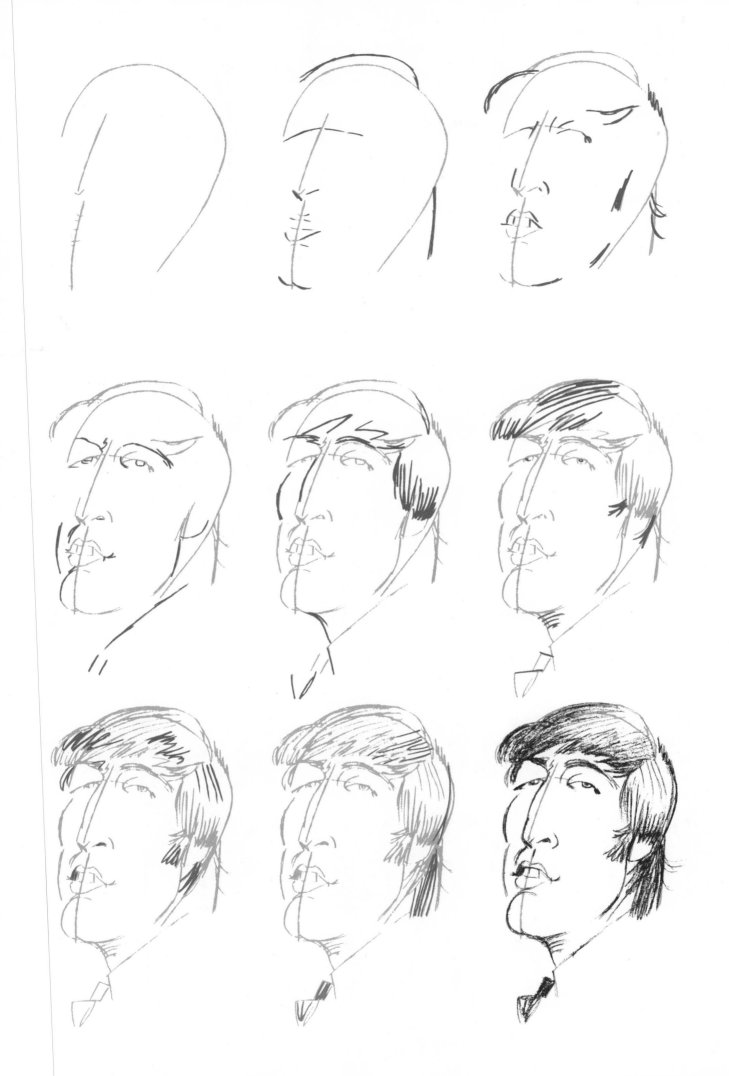

JOHN LENNON

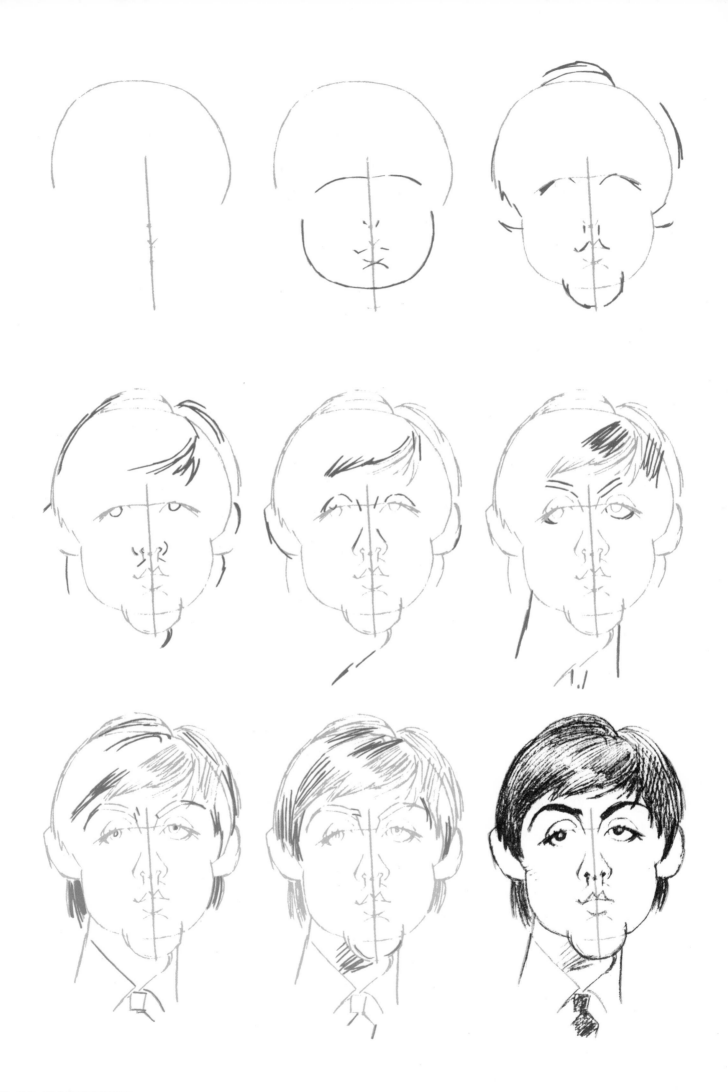

PAUL McCARTNEY

BETTE MIDLER

MADONNA

BILL COSBY

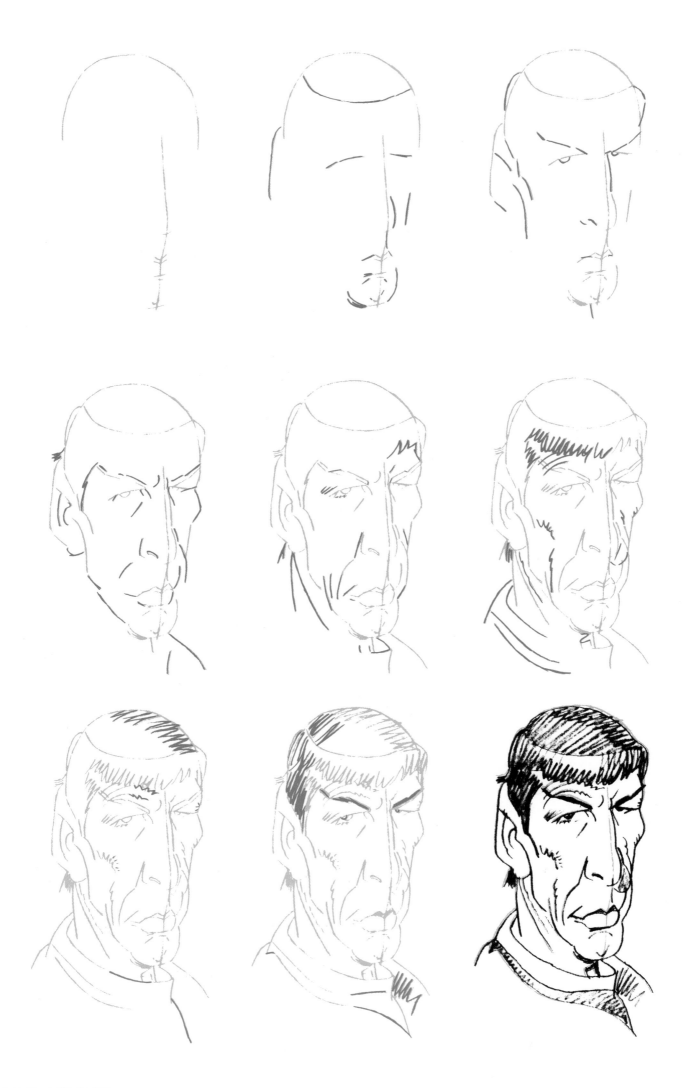

LEONARD NIMOY

BARBRA STREISAND

DARRYL STRAWBERRY

CHARLIE CHAPLIN

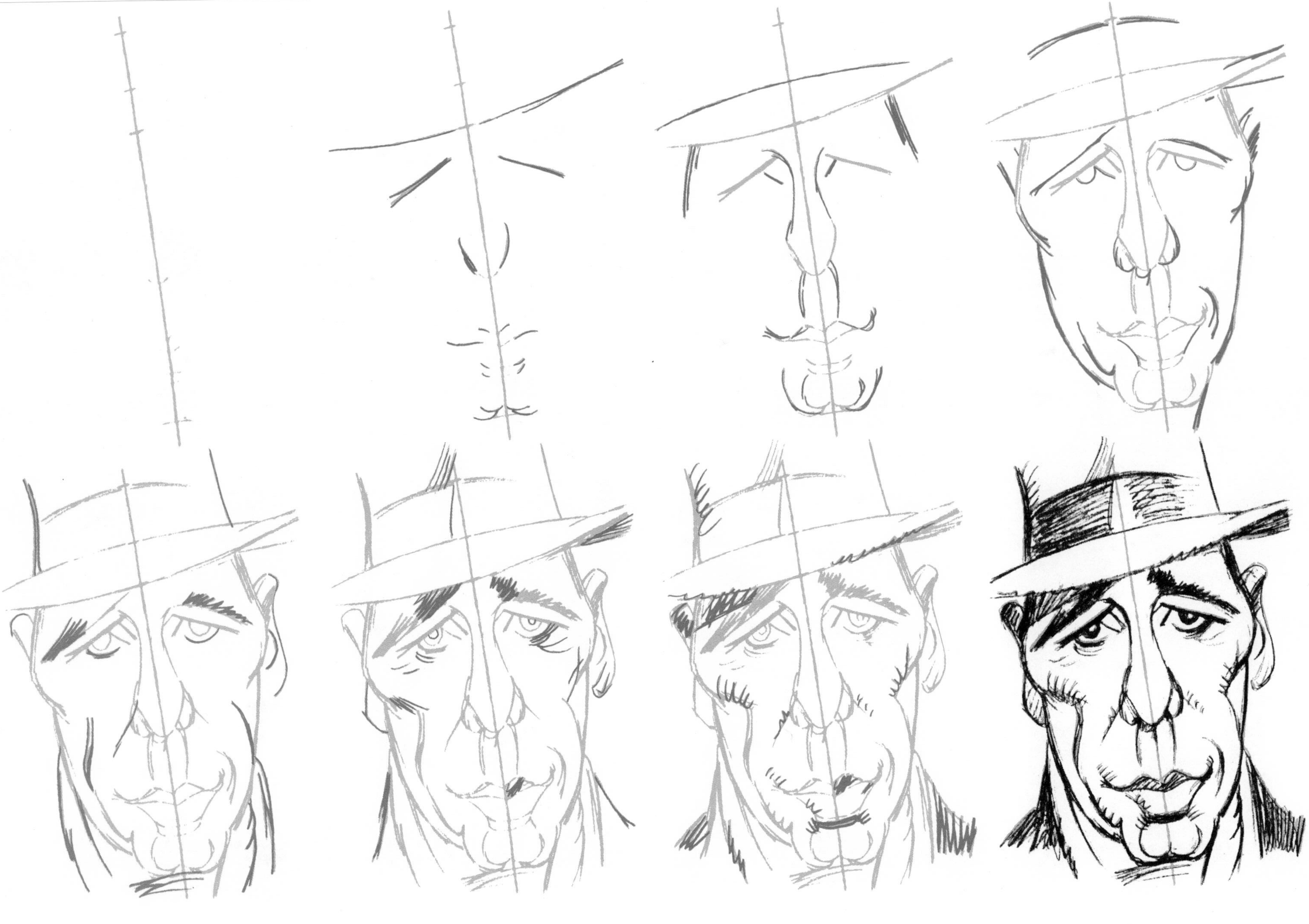

HUMPHREY BOGART

KATHARINE HEPBURN

PEE-WEE HERMAN

MICK JAGGER

LEE J. AMES has been "drawing 50" since 1974 when the first Draw 50 title—*Draw 50 Animals*—was published. Since that time, Ames has taught millions of people to draw everything from dinosaurs and sharks to boats, buildings, and cars. There are currently nineteen titles in the Draw 50 series and nearly two million books in print.

Ames divides his time between Long Island, New York—where he runs an art studio—and Southern California. At the moment, he is working on a new drawing series for very young children.

MORT DRUCKER has adorned *Mad* magazine with his original caricatures for thirty-five years. In addition, he has drawn more than a dozen covers for *Time* magazine, tackled assignments for nearly every major ad agency in the country, and published several of his own books, including *Familiar Faces: The Art of Mort Drucker*, a comprehensive biography which traces his nearly forty-year career. Director George Lucas has called him the "Leonardo da Vinci of cartoonists" while actor Michael J. Fox said, "I knew I had made it when Mort Drucker drew me."

Drucker was the recipient of the 1988 Reuben Award, the most prestigious award given in the field of cartooning.

He currently lives on Long Island, New York.